A

Siamese Cats

Loren Spiotta-DiMare

This book is dedicated,
with deepest love and admiration,
to my grandfather, Joseph Spiotta.

Color Photography

Donna J. Coss 18
Isabelle Francais 17, 19, 21; posters A,
B, and C
Dr. Robert C. Koestler 24, 58-top, 59,
60, 62, 63-top

Larry Levy 61
Olan Mills 22
Pet Library 23
Ron Reagan 57, 64

Distributed in the UNITED STATES by T.F.H. Publications, Inc., 211 West
Sylvania Avenue, Neptune City, NJ 07753; in CANADA by H & L Pet Supplies
Inc., 27 Kingston Crescent, Kitchener, Ontario N2B 2T6; Rolf C. Hagen Ltd.,
3225 Sartelon Street, Montreal 382 Quebec; in ENGLAND by T.F.H. Publica-
tions Limited, 4 Kier Park, Ascot, Berkshire SL5 7DS; in AUSTRALIA AND
THE SOUTH PACIFIC by T.F.H. (Australia) Pty. Ltd., Box 149, Brookvale
2100 N.S.W., Australia; in NEW ZEALAND by Ross Haines & Son, Ltd., 18
Monmouth Street, Grey Lynn, Auckland 2 New Zealand; in SINGAPORE
AND MALAYSIA by MPH Distributors (S) Pte., Ltd., 601 Sims Drive,
03/07/21, Singapore 1438; in the PHILIPPINES by Bio-Research, 5 Lippay
Street, San Lorenzo Village, Makati Rizal; in SOUTH AFRICA by Multipet
Pty. Ltd., 30 Turners Avenue, Durban 4001. Published by T.F.H. Publications
Inc. Manufactured in the United States of America by T.F.H. Publications,
Inc.

Contents

Poster A
Blue lynx point neuter owned by
Larry Levy.

Poster B
Seal lynx point neuter owned by
Nicole Ledoux.

Poster C
Blue point female and blue lynx point
neuter owned by Larry Levy.

Front cover photo by Isabelle Francais.

Introduction

Among the breeds of purebred cats, Siamese have always been and continue to be one of the most popular.

As a writer keenly interested in the welfare of all animals and the promotion of improved pet owner responsibility, I have written this book to acquaint the reader with all aspects of caring for and living with the Siamese cat. This elegant feline is unique in many ways. It has been my pleasure to investigate the history and nature of the Siamese, and it is my hope that you will enjoy learning about this breed as much as I have enjoyed writing this book for you.

As we go to press the Siamese cat is caught in the midst of a controversy regarding show color standards which will be discussed later. I have tried to present the information pertaining to this issue in an objective manner. As a writer it is my responsibility to bring pertinent information to the reader's attention, so he may draw his own conclusions.

Chapters dealing with health care and maintenance are presented only as a guide; they are not meant to replace the advice of a competent veterinarian.

History

The true ancestry of the Siamese cat is lost in antiquity. There are, of course, many different theories pertaining to its origin. Most are based on speculation romanticized by legend and fable. However, it is generally believed that the breed developed in Siam, an exotic Oriental nation, now known as Thailand.

Unlike other felines who may have had humble beginnings, the Siamese was born an aristocrat, owned by the King of Siam and held in very high esteem. Aside from this royal pet status, he is said to have guarded the palace, warning the King of intruders. The Siamese has a piercing cry, so it's not inconceivable that it really was employed as a "watchcat."

The Siamese also resided in Buddhist temples. Although there is no concrete evidence to prove it was involved in religious ceremonies, he has been referred to as the "sacred Siamese." The fact that Siamese kittens are born white, a color symbolizing purity, may have contributed to the use of this title. According to legend, the Siamese also acted as a guardian of the temples.

Only royalty and the wealthy were allowed to own Siamese cats. These animals were few in number due to a careful breeding program. Though there were Siamese-type cats roaming the streets and breeding freely, these were not of the same quality as the royal Siamese and should not be confused with them.

True Siamese cats were not given away indiscriminately. To be presented with a Siamese was to receive a prestigious gift. Just such a gift brought the Siamese to England. In 1884 the King of Siam gave British Consul-General Owen Gould a pair of his exquisite cats. They were exhibited a year later at the Crystal Palace in London. The breed became instantly popular.

The first Siamese came to America in 1890; supposedly they, too, were a gift from the King to an American friend. They were shown in the early 1900's, causing quite a stir in the cat fancy.

Appreciation of this uniquely attractive cat seems to know no bounds. Among all purebred cats today, the Siamese reigns

History

supreme. His pointed coat (darker markings on the mask, ears, legs, feet and tail) and tubular body type have captured the imagination of cat fanciers, many of whom have used the Siamese in their breeding programs to create new exotic breeds (much to the chagrin of purist Siamese breeders). The Siamese has contributed to the gene pool of the Balinese, Himalayan, Havana Brown, lilac Foreign Shorthair, Burmese, Oriental Shorthair, Tonkinese and the Russian Blue.

The Siamese was not always the sleek, fine-boned, long-legged cat with a wedge-shaped head and large ears that we know today. The original Siamese was much larger and stockier with a rounded head. It took years of selective breeding to create a svelte, elegant cat. However, the Siamese has retained his breathtakingly beautiful blue eyes and pointed coat. Squints (crossed eyes) and kinked tails still appear in the breed. Although some find these characteristics appealing, they are considered serious show faults. Yet these traits have been passed

down through generations—their origins based on fables.

Almost all Siamese fanciers can recount a story that explains the emergence of crossed eyes and kinked tails. A favorite is of the two cats, Chula and Tien, who lived in a remote temple with an elderly priest. When the priest died, the cats decided that Tien, the male, should go out and search for a new young priest, while Chula, the female, should guard the sacred chalice, the temple's one true treasure.

Chula became burdened by her duties; since she dared not leave the chalice unattended, she slept with her tail curled tightly around the stem of the cup. Thus, no one could steal the precious treasure without disturbing her. She spent her waking hours staring fixedly at the cup.

Weeks later Tien returned with a young priest. Subsequently Chula had a litter of kittens, all with kinked tails and crossed eyes due to Chula's prenatal preoccupation with "guard duty."

Another fable claims a princess placed her ring on her cat's tail,

The Siamese Cat

knotting the end to keep the ring from falling off. Yet another fable suggests the kink was caused by a forgetful Buddhist priest who knotted his cat's tail as a reminder to himself. Siamese cats are said to have had kinked tails ever after!

The Siamese head has become more of a long, tapering wedge (above), unlike the "apple heads" (below) of years ago.

According to the Cat Fanciers' Association, Inc. (CFA), the largest of the North American cat registering organizations, purebred cats fall into four classifications: Natural Breeds, Established Breeds, Mutations and Hybrids. For a cat to be considered a Natural Breed, the queen, stud and all ancestors must be of the same breed as the cat for whom registration is being sought.

Established breeds are created when two or more specified breeds have been mated. Once the new Established Breed exists, it can be continued by mating specimens of the new breed. Both the queen and stud of the cat seeking registration must be of the Established Breed. The pedigree may show specimens of the Established Breed and/or the other breeds used to create the Established Breed.

The mating of two or more breeds specified or unspecified in registration rules creates a Hybrid. Only breeds used to develop the Hybrid and/or specimens of the Hybrid Breed are allowed on the pedigree.

Mutations are the natural

offspring of a Natural Breed (for example, a shorthaired cat throws a kitten with long hair) that can be continued by mating specimens carrying the mutant gene and/or the original Natural Breed. The Siamese is considered a Natural Breed.

Not every feline registering association, foreign as well as North American, recognizes the same breeds for championship in show competition, and not all breeds are classified the same way by each association.

All associations have written show standards for each of the breeds they recognize for championship. A standard does not describe an actual cat but, rather, depicts an ideal cat, encompassing balance, proportion and harmony between individual parts. The standard describes the perfect cat, yet such a cat does not exist. Trying to breed a cat that reaches the standard is every breeder's dream, one which can never be completely fulfilled. Yet striving toward that goal is an ongoing challenge and perhaps the greater satisfaction. When cats compete in shows, they do not compete against each other but rather they compete against the standard.

The legs of the Siamese are long and slender, giving a graceful appearance.

Siamese cats are accepted in four colors by the CFA: Seal Point, Chocolate Point, Blue Point and Lilac Point. The latter three are mutations of the original Seal Point. However, within the last 50 years some breeders, intrigued with genetics and the possibility of expanding the range of Siamese colors, crossbred their cats with other breeds of the desired colors, usually American Shorthairs.

The Siamese Cat

Through careful selective breeding and linebreeding, they were able to refine these animals and establish unique varieties. Some of the new colors are truly exquisite. Yet this practice of crossbreeding Siamese with other breeds set off quite a furor with purist Siamese fanciers. Though these new cats are exactly like the original Siamese in type (structural appearance) and personality, staunch purists claim they are no longer a Natural Breed and should not be classified as Siamese. Thus in the CFA these cats are considered a breed unto themselves known as Colorpoint Shorthairs. In Britain and other North American organizations, however, they are accepted as Siamese.

No matter how they are classified, all are elegant, refined creatures. They actually have a sculptured appearance that would capture the eye of anyone with the slightest artistic inclination. Slender and graceful, Siamese/ Colorpoint Shorthairs carry themselves with dignity.

For the sake of comparison, the following are show standards taken from the CFA and the Cat Fanciers' Federation (CFF). In reviewing them you will discover differences as well as many similarities. [Please note: There are new color varieties of Siamese being developed which have not yet gained acceptance by the majority of associations, for example, the Cinnamon Point described in The International Cat Association's (TICA) Standards.]

CFA Siamese Standard

Point Score

HEAD (20)
   Long Flat Profile 6
   Wedge, Fine Muzzle, Size 5
   Ears 4
   Chin 3
   Width Between Eyes 2

EYES (10)
   Shape, Size, Slant and
     Placement 10

BODY (30)
   Structure and Size, Including
     Neck 12
   Muscle Tone 10
   Legs and Feet 5
   Tail 3

The Siamese Cat

COAT (10)

COLOR (30)

    Body Color 10
    Point Color (Matching Points
      of dense color, proper foot
      pads and nose leather) 10
    Eye Color 10

GENERAL: The ideal Siamese is a medium sized, svelte, refined cat with long tapering lines, very lithe but muscular. Males may be proportionately larger.

HEAD: Long tapering wedge. Medium size in good proportion to body. The total wedge starts at the nose and flares out in straight lines to the tips of the ears forming a triangle, with no break at the whiskers. No less than the width of an eye between the eyes. When the whiskers are smoothed back the underlying bone structure is apparent. Allowance must be made for jowls in the stud cat.

SKULL: Flat. In profile, a long straight line is seen from the top of the head to the tip of the nose. No bulge over eyes. No dip in nose.

EARS: Strikingly large, pointed, wide at base; continuing the lines of the wedge.

EYES: Almond shaped. Medium size. Neither protruding nor recessed. Slanted towards the nose in harmony with lines of the wedge and ears. Uncrossed.

NOSE: Long and straight. A continuation of the forehead with no break.

MUZZLE: Fine, wedge shaped.

CHIN AND JAW: Medium size. Tip of chin lines up with tip of nose in the same vertical plane. Neither receding nor excessively massive.

BODY: Medium size. Graceful, long and svelte. A distinctive combination of fine bones and firm muscles. Shoulders and hips continue same sleek lines of tubular body. Hips never wider than shoulders. Abdomen tight.

NECK: Long and slender.

The Siamese Cat

LEGS: Long and slim. Hind legs higher than front. In good proportion to body.

PAWS: Dainty, small, and oval. Toes, five in front and four behind.

TAIL: Long, thin, tapering to a fine point.

COAT: Short, fine textured, glossy. Lying close to body.

CONDITION: Excellent physical condition. Eyes clear. Muscular, strong, and lithe. Neither flabby nor boney. Not fat.

COLOR: Body: Even, with subtle shading when allowed. Allowance should be made for darker color in older cats as Siamese generally darken with age, but there must be definite contrast between body color and points. Points: Mask, ears, legs, feet, tail dense and clearly defined. All of the same shade. Mask covers entire face including whisker pads and is connected to ears by tracings. Mask should not extend over the top of the head. No ticking or white hairs in points.

PENALIZE: Improper (i.e., off-color or spotted) nose leather or paw pads. Soft or mushy body.

DISQUALIFY: Any evidence of illness or poor health. Weak hind legs. Mouth breathing due to nasal obstruction or poor occlusion. Emaciation. Visible kink. Eyes other than blue. White toes and/or feet. Incorrect number of toes. Malocclusion resulting in either undershot or overshot chin.

CFA Siamese Colors

SEAL POINT: Body even pale fawn to cream, warm in tone, shading gradually into lighter color on the stomach and chest. Points deep seal brown. Nose Leather and Paw Pads: Same color as points. Eye Color: Deep vivid blue.

CHOCOLATE POINT: Body ivory with no shading. Points milk-chocolate color, warm in tone. Nose leather and Paw Pads:

The Siamese Cat

Cinnamon-Pink. *Eye Color:* Deep vivid blue.

BLUE POINT: Body bluish white, cold in tone, shading gradually to white on stomach and chest. Points deep blue. *Nose Leather and Paw Pads:* Slate colored. *Eye Color:* Deep vivid blue.

LILAC POINT: Body glacial white with no shading. Points frosty grey with pinkish tone. *Nose Leather and Paw Pads:* Lavender-Pink. *Eye Color:* Deep vivid blue.

CFF Siamese Standard

Point Score

HEAD	15
EARS	5
EYES	8
EYE COLOR	8
NECK	2
BODY	10
TAIL	6
LEGS AND FEET	6
COAT	10
BODY COLOR	10
POINT COLOR	10
CONDITION	5
BALANCE	5

HEAD: Long tapering wedge starts at the nose and flares out in straight lines to the tips of the ears, forming a triangle with no break at the whiskers. Nose long and straight, a continuation of the forehead with no break. Skull flat. Muzzle fine and wedge shaped. Chin and jaw medium in size. Tip of chin lines up with the tip of the nose in the same vertical plane. No less than a width of an eye between the eyes. When whiskers are smoothed back, the underlying bone structure is apparent. Head medium in size, in good proportion to body. Objections: round or broad head, short or broad muzzle, bulge over eyes, dip in nose, receding or excessively massive chin.

EARS: Strikingly large, pointed, wide at the base, continuing with the lines of the wedge.

EYES: Almond shaped, medium sized, slanted upward toward the nose in harmony with the lines

The Siamese Cat

of the wedge. Objections: small, round or unslanted eye aperture, protruding or receding eyes.

EYE COLOR: Deep vivid blue. Objection: pale eye color.

NECK. Long and slender, carried to display the length. Objections: short or thick neck.

BODY: Medium sized, long and svelte. A distinctive combination of fine bones and firm muscles. Shoulders and hips continue the same sleek lines of the tubular body. Hips never wider than the shoulders, abdomen tight. Objections: cobby, short, thick or flabby body; belly pouch.

TAIL: Narrow at base, long, thin, tapering to a fine point, giving the effect of slenderness and length (tail, when brought down along the hind leg, should reach the tip of the foot, or when brought along the body should reach the shoulder). Tail to be in balance with size of the cat. Objections: thick base, non-tapering tail.

LEGS AND FEET: Legs long and slim, hind legs longer than the front legs, in good proportion to the body. Paws small and dainty. Objections: short legs, heavy leg bones, large or round feet.

COAT: Short, fine textured, glossy, lying close to the body. Withhold wins for: coats that have been sanded or shaved.

BODY COLOR: Even, with subtle shading when allowed. Allowances should be made for darker color in older cats as they generally darken with age, but there must be a definite contrast between body color and points. Objections: uneven body color or shading, dark spots on belly, hip spots.

POINT COLOR: Mask, ears, feet, legs and tail dense and clearly defined. All of the same shade. Mask covers entire face including whisker pads and is connected to the ears by tracings. Objections: complete hood; light hairs in points.

CONDITION: Hard and muscular, with no indication of

fat or emaciation. An appearance of good health and vitality.

BALANCE: A svelte cat with long tapering lines, very lithe, but muscular. Overall appearance of a well-balanced cat. Medium-sized cat, should not be too small or too large. Miniaturization to be considered a severe fault.

CFF Siamese Colors

RED POINT: Body clear white with any shading in the same tone as the points. Points—deep orange-red. Nose leather—flesh or coral pink. Paw pads—flesh or coral pink. Red is a slowly developing color, often requiring two years for full development of color intensity.

LYNX POINT: Mask—vertical stripes or intricate letter *M* on forehead; horizontal stripes on cheeks; dark spots at base of whiskers; bridge of nose may have a shading of gray or fawn gold. Ears—solid color, usually with a thumb mark of paler color on back of each ear. Nose leather —may be solid color, same as corresponding color of Siamese, or pink outlined in point color. Paw pads—to correspond with points. Legs—irregular bracelet bars of point color, the color being darkest on heels and the webbing of the toes. Allowance to be made for fainter point markings in young cats, particularly in Chocolate and Lilac. Tail—evenly barred in point color, tail tip ending in deepest point color (Seal with black tip; Chocolate with chocolate tip; Blue with dark blue tip; and Lilac with silvery-gray tip).

SEAL LYNX POINT: Stripes— dark seal brown or black. Ears— dark fawn to seal, shading to black at tips; may have paler fawn thumb marks. Body—cream or pale fawn, shading to lighter color on stomach and chest. Body shading may take form of ghost striping.

BLUE LYNX POINT: Stripes— blue gray. Ears—deep blue gray; may have thumb marks. Heels and tail tip—dark blue gray. Body bluish white to platinum gray, cold in tone, shading to lighter color on chest and stomach. Body shading may take form of ghost striping.

CHOCOLATE LYNX POINT: Stripes—warm cinnamon or milk chocolate. Ears—warm chocolate; may have paler thumb mark. Heels and tail tip deep warm chocolate. Body—ivory. Body shading may take form of ghost striping.

LILAC LYNX POINT: Stripes frosty gray with pinkish tone bars. Ears—frosty gray; may have paler thumb marks. Heels and tail tip—frosty gray. Body— glacial white. Body shading may take form of ghost striping.

RED LYNX POINT: Stripes— deep orange-red. Ears—deep orange-red; may have paler thumb marks. Heels and tail tip —deep orange-red. Body white. Body shading may take form of ghost striping.

TORTIE POINT: Color patching is restricted to points and should be mottled with clear bright patches of red and/or cream. Should not be brindled.

Both colors should appear in all points, particularly in the mask, and the characteristic blaze is highly desirable. Faint mottling allowed in body color of older cats. Footpads and nose leather to correspond to corresponding color of Siamese, but may have clear pink patching where point mottling extends into paw pads.

Seal Tortie Point: Points—deep seal brown, uniformly mottled with red and cream; a blaze is desirable. Body—pale fawn to cream, shading to lighter color on chest and stomach.

Chocolate Tortie Point: Points— warm cinnamon, uniformly mottled with cream; a blaze is desirable. Body—ivory, mottled in older cats.

Blue Tortie Point: Points—blue gray uniformly mottled with cream; a blaze is desirable. Body —bluish white to platinum gray, cold in tone, and shading to a lighter tone on the chest and stomach. May be mottled in older cats.

Lilac Tortie Point: Points— frosty gray, uniformly mottled with cream; a blaze is desirable. Body—glacial white, may be mottled in older cats.

The Siamese Cat

(NOTE: Chocolate, Lilac and Blue Tortie Points may be uniformly mottled with both red and cream in the points.)

CREAM POINT: Body—clear white with any shading in the same tone as the points. Points—apricot. Nose leather—flesh to coral pink. Paw pads—flesh to coral pink.

SEAL POINT: Points—deep seal brown. Body—even pale fawn to cream, warm in tone, shading gradually into lighter color on the chest and stomach. Nose leather and paw pads—deep seal brown or black.

CHOCOLATE POINT: Points—milk chocolate, warm in tone. Body—ivory with no shading. Nose leather and paw pads—cinnamon pink.

BLUE POINT: Points—deep blue. Body—bluish white, cold in tone, shading gradually to white on chest and stomach. Nose leather and paw pads to be slate gray color.

LILAC POINT: Points—frosty gray with pinkish tone. Body color—glacial white with no shading. Nose leather and paw pads—lavender pink.

Captions for color photos on pages 17-24.
Page 17: The Siamese standard calls for a head that is a long and tapering wedge, similar to that of Champion Petmark's Mischief Maker of Sengen. This seal lynx point neuter is owned by Nicole Ledoux. Page 18: Champion Cherry Garden Orpheus of Ellian, a male cinnamon lynx point and the first male of his color in the United States. Owner, Linda Kochis. Page 19: A blue lynx point neuter, Supreme Grand Champion B-Jay's Looney Tunes, owned by Larry Levy. Page 20: Eloise I. Trosan's two companions, Luzerne's Lexington and CFA Champion Luzerne's Peerless, are nine-month-old lilac points. They love warmth, and since the fireplace is a great source of curiosity for them, they need to be watched carefully. Page 21: This blue point female, Double Grand Champion B-Jay's Blue Ice of Petmark, exhibits the long, flat profile so characteristic of show-quality Siamese bred today. Owner, Larry Levy. Page 22: Stephanie Berwanger holds Ellian Pandora N. of Bergattos, a cinnamon point owned by Liesel Berwanger. Page 23: Cats and dogs, in this case a seal point Siamese and a Basset Hound, can grow to be the greatest of friends. Page 24: Dr. Robert C. Koestler's seal point male, Miyo Mid-Nite Express of Saroko.

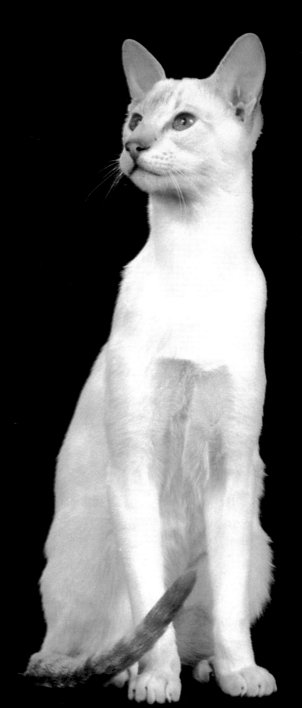

Buying a Siamese Cat

Once you have decided the Siamese is the breed for you, how do you go about finding one? A little investigative research is essential. As with the selection and purchase of any animal, the informed fancier becomes a knowledgeable buyer.

Your goal is to find a reputable Siamese breeder. You can begin your search by contacting the CFA or one of the other feline registries. If you request a list of breeders in your local area or state, many of these organizations will be able to provide you with one. Some people buy their pets from quality breeders in distant states, relying on the breeders' choice of the kitten best suited to the buyer's specifications. Although this is a perfectly acceptable practice, I prefer to visit the breeder myself, interact with a litter and make my own selection. This way I can observe the parents (not always both, but at least the mother) and the environment. In addition, I don't think anything quite surpasses the joy and excitement of choosing that special little someone. Or, as is so often the case, a certain someone selects you!

Do not feel obligated to buy a kitten from the first breeder you visit. In fact it is best to visit as many as possible, comparing litters, asking questions and so on. This is an important decision; you want to make the right choice. Most breeders will agree to let a buyer take his new purchase to a veterinarian of his own choosing. If for some reason the kitten is found to be unhealthy in any way upon examination, the buyer has the right to return his purchase for a refund or to make another selection. Of course, these agreements vary from breeder to breeder and from state to state, so it makes good sense to find out what the details are well in advance.

Another good source to utilize is *Cats* Magazine, a publication which has an extensive list of breeders.

Cat shows also present a perfect opportunity to observe and learn. If you see a cat that appeals to you, by all means speak to the owners. They may well have litters waiting for new homes or on the way. When

Buying a Siamese Cat

making inquiries at shows, do use some discretion. Although your enthusiasm may get the better of you, don't ask an owner about his cats while they are being judged or being groomed for judging. Wait for a more opportune moment when the owner is relaxed and open to questions. For those involved, shows are very important and often nerve-racking. Most breeders would love to talk about their cats; timing is important, however. Be considerate—your thoughtfulness will be appreciated.

Catteries or small private breeders specializing in Siamese are best. That is not to say breeders with one or two other breeds should be avoided. In fact many dedicated cat fanciers can't resist having more than one breed. You should be able to see the difference between these people and commercial breeders. The dedicated fancier raises cats for love of the animal; profit, if there is any to be made, is of secondary importance.

Any cat lover should not pass up the opportunity to visit a cattery. Though the uninformed may be distressed to see cats in cages, there is no need for alarm. Breeders' opinions differ on the use of cages. However, adapting to a cage is part of the show cat's life. If given additional exercise, play periods and plenty of attention, the cattery cat will be content. Of course proper diet and clean living quarters are essential. Catteries usually have large play areas. To see twenty or so cats of the breed you adore romping together defies description.

Many reputable catteries and small-scale breeders don't need to advertise. Their reputations precede them. They often have waiting lists for their kittens; sometimes kittens are sold even before they're born. Veterinarians, especially those specializing in cats, may be able to put you in touch with breeders. Many pet shops also have referral services.

People who buy cats usually fall into three categories: those who want pets, those who want breeding stock or those who want show cats. You should decide just what it is you're looking for beforehand. That way the breeder will best be able to help

Buying a Siamese Cat

you make the right choice. He should be happy to answer your questions regarding the kitten's background, bloodlines, personality, etc. If you buy a pet-quality kitten, don't feel you are accepting an inferior animal. Sometimes the difference between the show cat and the pet is so miniscule that it is noticeable only to the trained eye. Buying a pet-quality kitten in no way decreases the animal's value as a pet, though the price will be affected.

If you are only interested in having a pet, it should be altered. This will eliminate the adult female's high-pitched calling and the male's natural spraying habit, both of which can be quite intolerable. Altered cats usually make better pets. Some breeders insist that the pet-quality kittens they sell be spayed or neutered. Besides producing a more agreeable companion, altering eliminates the possibility of unplanned parenthood.

Dedicated Siamese breeders take the placing of their kittens in good homes very seriously. Many literally "interview"

prospective buyers. Don't be offended if you feel you're being given the third degree; keep in mind that the breeder has a lot of time, love (and money) invested in his cats and wants only the best for them.

Some breeders insist that their cats remain indoors; walking in a harness or romping in a backyard enclosed gazebo is acceptable, but running free is definitely not. Some strongly oppose declawing and will not sell their kittens to those who plan to declaw.

One breeder I know asks buyers who already have a cat at home to have that one tested for feline leukemia virus (FeLV). She requests written proof from a veterinarian stating that the cat is FeLV-negative. Then, and only then, will she allow the buyer to take one of her kittens home. This is a woman who places her cats' health and welfare above all else.

Prices for Siamese kittens vary according to area. Show-quality specimens will be priced higher than pet-quality animals; however, one must remember that although prices may seem high, these really don't begin to

Buying a Siamese Cat

cover the breeder's expenses. The breeder must keep the mother cat healthy by feeding her additional amounts of food during pregnancy and lactation, provide food for the kittens for at least three months, have them tested for FeLV, and pay for the kittens' inoculations.

If you see an advertisement for inexpensively priced Siamese kittens, they may be of mixed heritage, or they may not have received all of their inoculations. Though you may spend less money on these animals initially, you could be buying a big dose of heartache. Purchasing a healthy, genetically sound cat is worth the investment.

Siamese kittens, unlike puppies, should not be purchased until they are three to four months old, as they are unusually small to begin with and need time to build up their resistance to disease. Also, they should receive their inoculations at four, seven, ten and fourteen weeks to insure immunity against disease.

Siamese kittens go through several periods of development and need a suitable amount of time to become properly socialized. The mother weans her kittens at about eight weeks, at which point they begin to share the mother's food and use a litter pan. From six to eight weeks they are basically interested in their mother. At about seven to nine weeks they begin to interact with each other. Then, at about ten to twelve weeks, they start to realize that people offer more than food and they roam farther from their initial surroundings in search of human companionship. At this stage, the breeder will teach the kittens about manners, i.e., no climbing up curtains, jumping on tables, scratching furniture. The rate of development can not be hurried. If a kitten is taken from its secure environment before it is ready, it may be antisocial, unable to adapt to a new family, and, in general, become an inferior pet. In addition, as kittens mature, breeders are better able to determine if they are pet or show quality.

Caring breeders like to keep up with their kittens; in a sense they become an "extended family." You should always feel comfortable calling your breeder after you have purchased a kitten if you have questions or need advice. A reputable breeder will be happy to talk to you, and in fact probably looks forward to it. As one such breeder said to me, "I get the most wonderful Christmas cards from people I've sold my kittens to and I don't even celebrate Christmas!"

The Siamese is an emotional animal which thrives on human attention. Unlike other felines who prefer the solitary life and are content with an occasional petting from their owners, the Siamese is constantly underfoot. Kittens raised with love and affection become devoted to their owners and feel it necessary to constantly remind them of the fact. Your Siamese will follow you from room to room and when you stop to rest, will leap into your lap, settling down comfortably. If your pet feels he is being ignored, he may lick or nip your fingers in order to get your attention.

There may be times when you don't want this devoted bundle of fur in your lap, but it makes no difference—he wants to be with you! If he's banished to another room, he will loudly cry his protest until someone gives in. That will probably be you!

The Siamese has all the endearing traits of other felines, and more. To cat lovers this intensified personality makes him a most desirable companion. Even non-cat fanciers are often taken with the Siamese once

Personality

they've had the pleasure of interacting with one. Because of their loyalty and devotion, Siamese should be owned only by those who will appreciate their ingratiating natures. A highly sensitive animal, the Siamese would suffer greatly if ignored.

This breed is known to be extremely active and curious. They are the "clowns" of the cat world who love to run and leap for no reason other than the simple joy of it. They create their own games and love you to join in. Their curiosity often leads them into mischief, especially since they are very adept at opening doors (linen closets, cabinets, etc.), as well as containers. If your pet hears you opening the refrigerator door, he will stop what he's doing and appear at your feet to help you investigate. Always be careful not to trap your cat in the refrigerator or a closet. It could cause you both undue stress.

Though Siamese have been referred to as "dog-like" in their never-ending pursuit of human companionship, they have also been likened to monkeys because of their intelligence, slim physique, quick movements and exploring hands (paws). If you prefer a more sedate companion, the Siamese is not for you.

People who live in a multiple cat breed household claim the Siamese never seems to become as lethargic in the reclining years as other breeds. Of course, we all slow down to some degree as we get older, but the Siamese behaves like the "eternal kitten" and seems to retain his "joie de vivre."

Because of their sensitive natures, Siamese have an uncanny ability to recognize their owners' moods in a way which is unparalleled by other breeds. If you're blue, your pet will do his best to cheer you. If you feel like being quiet and reflective, he too will settle down. Then, again, if you are extremely irritable and cannot be consoled, he has the sense to stay out of your way!

Although I have emphasized the breed's active nature, the Siamese also has the ability to adapt to his owner's lifestyle. For example, he will slow down the pace if he lives with elderly people. One older woman who owns two Siamese cats can't have them running about while she's cooking, as she fears she'll trip over them. Therefore, they have been trained to wait patiently on two stools in the kitchen while she cooks. They remain there until given the command to get down. They also know *their* dinner will not be served unless they behave.

There has been much talk lately about the benefits of pet therapy, animals interacting with the elderly, the infirm or the handicapped to help to boost the morale of those who may be giving up on life. Siamese make excellent pet therapists. They seem to have endless patience and adore the extra petting and attention.

In general, the Siamese, if they have been properly socialized, will act favorably with strangers. Those that have not may run away in fear, but a well-socialized cat will greet a guest with active curiosity. If you're going to obtain your kitten from a cattery, note how the cats react to you. If you are greeted at the door by a troop of inquisitive kittens and cats, this is definitely a good sign. Kittens raised in a cattery should be allowed out of their cages for extended play periods in the house, enabling them to interact with family and friends.

Siamese get along well with children, particularly if they have been raised with them. Of course rambunctious children would frighten any animal. Be careful not to expose your cat to any potentially harmful situations. It would be best to supervise children who come to visit, as even the most gentle child might inadvertently harm your pet. For the most part, Siamese love attention from whoever offers it.

Because Siamese thrive on companionship, it would be unfair to leave one alone all day. If you work, or are away a good deal of the time, it would be best to buy a companion for your pet —preferably another Siamese!

Different Colors-Different Personalities?

Opinions differ on this question. If you asked a hundred knowledgeable Siamese breeders to describe personality

Personality

differences among the various colors, you'd probably get a hundred different answers. For example, some might say the Seal Points are generally more loving and have the most even temperament, while others would claim the Seals are very high strung. Still others would say a Siamese is a Siamese—color has nothing at all to do with personality or temperament. Certainly each breeder would have his own personal preference as to the best-natured Siamese.

Because concerned breeders spend a good deal of time watching their kittens grow and develop individual personalities, you'd be wise to look for a color that strikes your fancy. Then ask the breeder to tell you about each kitten's personality. Remember too, your interaction with your pet will affect the way he behaves as he matures.

While each cat is a unique individual, the Siamese in general are fun-loving, affectionate, outgoing animals—a true joy to own.

The Siamese Voice

The Siamese, notoriously known (by some) for its raucous voice, definitely has a talkative nature. It is in fact one of his distinctive characteristics. If he wants something, he wants it *now* and clearly vocalizes his desires. If he is ignored, he will howl loudly for attention. Actually, his voice encompasses a wide range of sounds and has an almost human-like quality. Those dedicated to the breed find his talking ability quite endearing, declaring, "You can have a true conversation with a Siamese." Neighbors, especially those in close quarters, may not share the Siamese fancier's enthusiasm.

An adult male's voice can carry a great distance. The female, when in heat, screams like a banshee. Neutering the pet Siamese will stifle these amorous cries. Though the howling will subside, your pet will still enjoy talking to you. Learn to listen to him. His communication skills can be quite fascinating and will help you better understand him, creating a stronger bond between the two of you.

Your New Kitten

For years, cats have been regarded as third class citizens. Purchased on the spur of the moment by those who haven't taken the time to anticipate their needs, cats have often been misunderstood, mistreated, neglected, or abandoned. Animal shelters throughout the country are filled with unwanted cats and kittens, many of whom face certain death.

Although cats today are held in higher esteem, irresponsible pet ownership still exists. If you are determined to own a purebred cat, are prepared to pay the higher costs, and have made the effort to research the various bloodlines, you will probably take good care of your pet. However, before actually purchasing your kitten, give the following questions serious consideration.

Do you want a nice pet?

A kitten with show potential?

A show-quality kitten, even though you have no intention of showing it?

(Because breeders spend a good deal of time and money improving their bloodlines, they may be hesitant to sell a show-quality kitten to someone who does not plan to show.)

A male or female?

A cat for breeding purposes?

One kitten, or two?

As you can see, buying a cat is not a simple matter, as there is much to decide. Once you have focused on the cat you want and can responsibly care for, then you can select your kitten.

What to Look For

Presumably you have chosen a cattery or small-scale breeder with clean facilities and healthy, happy, well-socialized cats. Ideally, you should be looking at a litter with four-month-old kittens. (You may select a kitten at a younger age and return when it is old enough to go to a new home.)

Watch the kittens carefully as they interact with each other and you. Be sure to select one that is in obvious good health—playful and lively. His eyes should be clear, his coat smooth and finely textured and, though he is small, he should feel solid. Signs of ill-health include eyelids that are

33

Your New Kitten

half-shut, watery eyes, runny nose, unsightly coat, diarrhea and overall sluggish manner. If the kitten you've fallen in love with appears ill, pass him over. Trouble at a young age could mean greater heartbreak later on. It's better to start out with a kitten who is happy and well.

Environment

Undoubtedly there will be much excitement for old and young alike when you bring home the new feline member of the family. But for the kitten's sake, it's best for everyone to stay as calm as possible. For the drive home, your kitten should be placed in a carrier or cardboard box lined with a soft blanket—not a good one, as it might get soiled.

Be sure to have the kitten's room or living area set up before he arrives. It should be a quiet spot to help him feel secure, but it should not be totally isolated. If possible, place the litter box nearby, but no matter where you place it, keep it there permanently.

Your kitten will be frightened and unsure of himself, all alone away from his mother, littermates and familiar surroundings. Even though you will eventually become the center of his world, he doesn't know this yet. So to make the transition easier, hold down the noise and excitement and don't handle him too much. If you must pick the kitten up, do so properly by placing one hand under his chest and one under his hindquarters. *Never* lift him by the scruff of his neck. Make sure he is not exposed to drafts or drastic temperature changes. Don't feed him any bones.

The first night he will certainly cry out. Don't run to comfort him as this is negative reinforcement. You may place an alarm clock in or near his bed; the ticking, which might remind him of his mother's heartbeat, may comfort him. A warm water bottle placed in his bed may also help. He'll settle down in a few days.

If you have other pets, don't introduce them to the new kitten until he has been checked by your veterinarian and has become

Your New Kitten

somewhat accustomed to his new home. It is not advisable to bring a new kitten into your house unless you are certain he is free of feline leukemia virus (FeLV), a highly contagious feline disease.

A Siamese brought up in a calm environment will develop into a calm, happy cat. However, because this breed is so sensitive, they tend to take on some of the personality traits of their owners. Highly nervous people may find they are living with a nervous, high-strung cat. Try to act in a sedate manner around your pet— you may find he actually helps you relax.

Names

If you buy a purebred Siamese you should acquire his pedigree; even if you don't plan to show, it's nice to have, and you may be bitten by the show bug later on.

A cat must be registered in order to be shown. Registered cats can have two names, their proper name (which appears on the pedigree and includes the cattery name), and their pet name. Of course, a pet name can be a shortened version of the proper name.

For example: Proper Name— SiLing's Ebony Mist. Shortened Version—Ebony or Misty. Pet Name— Topper.

There are different methods for registering a kitten, depending on whether his litter has been registered as a group or each kitten has been registered individually. Your breeder should give you the necessary information.

There is an entire psychology behind what people choose to name their pets. What you choose to name your cat gives an interesting insight into your personality and feelings toward your pet. A cat christened "Useless" says much about his owner.

Since you have gone to the extent of buying a purebred cat and narrowed it down further by selecting a regal breed such as the Siamese, why not give your pet a royal name? There are several Pet Name books available which may be of help. Or if you want to select a name unique to the cat's ancestry, why not get

Feeding

hold of a Thai/English dictionary? Whatever you decide to do, name your cat as soon as possible so he will be able to make the association between the word and himself, thereby beginning to form a bond of communication between the two of you.

Because there are so many commercial pet foods on the market today, making the proper choice may seem like a difficult task. Of course, you should discuss diet with your breeder before you pick up your kitten and bring him into your home. This way you can purchase the kitten's food prior to his arrival. The breeder may give you a small supply to last for the first few days. In either case, it's important to feed your new kitten the diet he is accustomed to. A drastic change will cause digestive upset, which will only add to the stress he is certain to feel away from his mother and littermates.

Kittens should be fed four times a day until they are six months old; from that point on, twice a day will suffice. If you wish to change your cat's diet as he ages, you may, but do so gradually. A sudden change in diet at any age can upset the digestive system.

When you are faced with a seemingly endless row of commercial pet foods in your grocery store, there are a few guidelines you ought to follow to

Feeding

make the right choice. First, you'll want to select a product which contains all the nutrients (protein, fat, carbohydrate, vitamins and minerals) a cat needs to remain fit. Read labels carefully. Look for words like: "100% nutritionally complete" or "complete and balanced nutrition." These phrases indicate that the products were accepted as nutritionally complete by the National Academy of Sciences—National Research Council (NRC) and/or the American Association of Feed Control Officials (AAFCO). Those that are not so labeled are supplements and should be fed as such, or not at all. However, there are a few exceptions. Some pet food products meet the standards for a nutritionally complete diet but are not so labeled. If you are uncertain, and wish to pursue the matter further, you can write the manufacturer and ask if their products meet NRC standards.

Your next consideration is the type of food to select. You have three choices: 1) canned (moist), 2) semi-moist, 3) dry. Each type has advantages and disadvantages as explained below.

Canned foods are the most expensive and have a high water content. These products must be refrigerated after opening and then brought to room temperature before serving. Also, they do not help fight tartar build-up on the teeth. However, they are probably the most palatable and have the greatest flavor variety.

Semi-moist foods usually cost less than the canned foods, though the difference is often marginal. They are convenient to use and store. They're somewhat more palatable than the dry type and have less odor than the canned food. Many cats seem to like semi-moist products.

Dry foods are the least expensive of the three. They are convenient to use (they can be left out as part of a "self-feeding" plan, whereby your cat can feed whenever he wants to) and easy to store. This type helps to keep teeth and gums in good shape. Water should always be available for your Siamese, especially when dry foods are fed.

Feeding

The choice is basically up to you; however, you may wish to ask your veterinarian or breeder for advice on what type of food to offer your pet. I feel that a mixture of moist and dry, or semi-moist and dry, will cover all bases. *Never* feed your cat dog food. Cats have a need for higher protein and fat than dog foods provide.

Table Scraps

Feeding an exclusive diet of table scraps is not recommended. No matter how much care you take in preparing homemade meals, they may not be 100% nutritionally complete. Supplementing a commercial diet with 10-15% table scraps is acceptable. Use common sense; never feed anything to your cat you wouldn't eat yourself. Also, don't feed a cat spicy foods. Use the following as a guide when offering table scraps.

Meat—Roast beef, steak, stewing beef, beef kidney, beef liver, chicken liver, de-boned chicken and turkey.

Meat should always be cooked. Never serve raw meat, as it can cause loose stools or toxoplasmosis (a disease which can be transmitted to humans).

Fish—A tidbit of fish fed occasionally is o.k.

Vegetables—All vegetables are acceptable. Some cats adore tomatoes.

Dairy—Cottage cheese, plain yogurt, raw egg yolk. Raw egg whites are not good for cats; cooked eggs are acceptable.

Milk, despite popular belief, is not required in a cat's diet; in fact cow's milk can cause loose stools and is hard for some cats to digest. You may offer powdered milk if you like.

Vitamins—Siamese would do well with a good multiple vitamin. Vitamins are available in dry or syrup form.

Everyone has heard the expression "finicky cat" and often erroneously believes this characteristic is just part of a cat's nature. Finicky cats aren't born, they evolve, especially if they have weak-willed owners. Cats must learn that their meals will be fed at certain times of the

Feeding

day and should be eaten at those times. Don't spoil your cat. Place his food down in the same spot at the same time every day (he'll appreciate the routine). Leave the food there for fifteen minutes only and then remove it, even if it has only been partially eaten or not touched at all. A cat will not perish if he misses a meal or two. He will soon learn he must eat when his food is offered or he won't have another opportunity. Of course, use this procedure only for adult cats; kittens should be allowed to eat as much as possible. The same holds true for a sick cat.

Moist and semi-moist food should never be left to sit for hours, as this is an unsanitary and unhealthy practice. Dry food may safely be left out. However, a diet limited solely to dry food may be too high in calories. Consult your veterinarian if you are interested in a self-feeding program.

Many people think Siamese appear too "skinny" as a result of being starved, which simply isn't true. The Siamese, through years of careful breeding, was designed to be a slender, graceful cat, which, to those unfamiliar with the breed, may seem skinny. A healthy Siamese is a firm, well-muscled, slender creature. If you run your hand over a cat's back and can feel his backbone, then he is too thin. A heavy cat is just as unhealthy as one that is underfed. Be sure to give your pet rations which match his body type. An average healthy female Siamese should weigh between six and eight pounds, a male between eight and ten pounds.

Many cats become accustomed to one brand or type of food and refuse to touch anything else. It's good practice to introduce some variety into your cat's diet early on. If he should become ill and require a special diet, he may refuse to eat it if he is unaccustomed to variety; this could become a life-threatening situation—perhaps more harmful than the actual illness.

A pet owner should control his cat's diet and eating habits, not the other way around. What you do for your pet, you do in his best interest. Keep this in mind when your cat tries some nearly irresistible feline tactic to get his own way.

Grooming

All short-haired cats are fairly easy to groom—the Siamese especially, because he has a very short fine coat. However, to keep him looking his best you should plan to give him a good brushing once a week. A rubber brush is excellent for gently removing dead hair, but don't get carried away as you may take out live hair as well.

Between weekly brushings, you may wish to go over your pet with a chamois or your hand. The oils of your skin will help to maintain the soft, easily managed coat.

The Siamese is a fastidious animal with no "catty" odor. He will keep himself clean and do a good job of it at that. But it is worthwhile for you to help him out occasionally, especially during warm weather when he'll shed more profusely. During the shedding season, there is also a higher risk of hairballs forming in his stomach, so increased grooming at this time is a good preventive measure. Siamese love to be brushed!

Aside from brushing, you should clip your cat's front claws once a week. Since the back claws wear off more rapidly, they can be clipped less often. You can buy a nail clipper designed for cats at most pet shops. Clip nails carefully, being careful not to cut into the quick (fleshy part under nail), as this will be painful and could cause infection. Your vet can show you how to do this properly.

For the most part your cat should not need a bath. But if he has really gotten himself dirty, a bath may be in order. He probably won't be thrilled with the idea, so work quickly and efficiently, using a shampoo made specifically for cats and available at most pet shops. Be careful not to get soap in his eyes or mouth. Use lukewarm water and rinse thoroughly. Then, with a large towel, dry him well.

There are many liquid shampoos as well as dry shampoos for cats on the market. Don't gamble with a product made for dogs *and* cats.

Because show cats must dazzle the judges, grooming to prepare for a show can be a little more extensive. All in all though, the Siamese is relatively easy to maintain in peak condition.

Grooming

Eyes

Cats may get bits of discharge caught in the corners of their eyes just as humans do. These should be removed gently with a cotton swab.

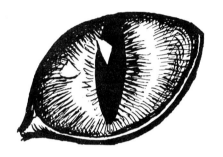

The eyes of the Siamese are almond shaped and medium in size.

Ears

Check the ears periodically for wax or signs of infection. If wax is present, remove it gently and carefully with a cotton swab which has been moistened with mineral oil. If anything else that seems out of the ordinary appears in the ear, consult your veterinarian.

Teeth

If dry cat food is part of his main diet, there should be no problems with his teeth. If it is not, your veterinarian should check the cat's teeth and gums regularly.

Fleas

Fleas are a true nuisance to both the cat and the cat owner. The thought of a flea-infested home is not a pleasant one. You can protect your pet by having him wear a flea collar designed for cats. Again, avoid preparations created for dogs. If the fleas have already settled in the house, vacuum frequently and sprinkle flea powder under rugs and furniture cushions. If the problem gets out of hand, you may have to hire a professional exterminator to rid your house of fleas.

Declawing

Declawing is quite a controversial issue in the cat

Training

world today. Some authorities insist declawing can cause surgical and post-operative complications, including continual pain, and can alter the cat's behavior in a negative manner, causing problems such as biting, or missing the litter pan. Those in favor of declawing claim it is a relatively simple and safe procedure and causes no negative side effects whatsoever. Still others feel if you must declaw, only the front claws should be removed, leaving the back claws intact to allow the cat some means of defense.

I must emphasize that many Siamese breeders are against declawing and will not sell their kittens to those who plan on having it done. Because Siamese are so intelligent, breeders feel they can easily learn to use a scratching post, arguing further that those who declaw just won't take the time to teach their cats to use the post. Because all pets require a certain degree of attention and training, prospective Siamese owners should consider beforehand how much time they are willing to devote to training their cat.

A well-mannered pet is a joy to own; an ill-mannered pet is a nuisance. Cats are no exception. Every cat-owning household should have a set of rules for its feline member to follow. Siamese owners are at an advantage due to the fact that their breed is exceptionally intelligent and possesses a great desire and willingness to please. Siamese cats are easily trained to follow house rules. They can also learn additional entertaining tricks if you care to extend their lessons.

The key to training a Siamese lies in being firm and consistent. Because this breed is so very sensitive, one should NEVER resort to any harsh treatment or violence. When teaching a Siamese a certain behavior, use consistent correction techniques. Don't let your cat get away with something "just this once." Although pets can turn on some beguiling looks, don't allow yourself to succumb to them, as you will only confuse the animal and defeat your training efforts. Only by your being consistent will your cat learn to understand what is expected of him.

Training

Never strike your cat with your hand. He should learn to think of your hand as a source of comfort and affection. Because cats dislike loud noises, you may clap your hands together with the simultaneous verbal correction, "No!", or, if warranted, roll a section of a newspaper together and crack it against the counter top or floor, again using the word "No!" This will certainly get your cat's attention. In time you may be able to do away with the hand clapping or newspaper. The word no should suffice.

Another good disciplinary tool is a water pistol or water spray bottle. If you catch your cat clawing the furniture, chewing a plant, or involved in some other misdeed, give him a good squirt and say "No!" He will get the message after a few such incidents. After a while a cat corrected with a water pistol or a squirt from a spray bottle can usually be kept in line by simply showing him the offensive spraying device.

Never tease your kitten. Though his pawing reactions may be cute at the time, as a mature cat, his striking claw can inflict a painful wound. The Siamese has an unfair and untrue reputation for being nasty. A vicious cat in all probability has been mistreated or improperly socialized. Children raised with Siamese, or any animal for that matter, should be taught to be gentle and never be allowed to tease or annoy the family pet.

The Litter Box

If you have acquired your kitten at the proper age, he should have learned from his mother to use the litter box (with a little help from the breeder) in his previous home. Probably all that will be necessary is for you to show the kitten where his litter box will be placed. Keep the box in the same area at all times so your kitten won't become confused. Be sure to clean the litter frequently. A Siamese will look at a dirty litter box with disdain, and possibly refuse to use it. In the beginning, use the same litter the kitten was accustomed to at the breeder's. If you wish to change the brand or

Training

type of litter at a later date, do so gradually.

Since nobody's perfect, your kitten may have a few accidents. All he needs is a gentle reminder. Put him into his litter pan and dig a small hole with your hand or with his paw. He'll soon recall his early training.

Scratching Post

Scratching posts are a must. Buy the tallest one you can find, or if you're handy, build your own. Be sure the base of the post is wide enough to keep it from falling over. The post itself, wrapped with carpeting, should be tall enough to allow the adult cat to stretch to his full capacity. Not only will the post help your cat exercise his muscles, but also it is the only acceptable outlet for his climbing and clawing instincts. As with the litter box, all you really need do is to introduce your cat to his post; he'll get the idea.

Because you'll want to make your pet as happy as possible, you may wish to make or purchase a more elaborate post.

There are models that reach from floor to ceiling with resting shelves, cubbyholes, etc. Your cat will love this kind of post and you will have the satisfaction of knowing how much you've contributed to his contentment.

Furniture and Curtain Clawing Prevention

While you have introduced your kitten to his litter box and scratching post, you should also be teaching your pet not to claw on curtains, carpeting, or furniture. Your breeder has possibly already begun this training, yet you may have to reinforce the lessons. Even with a scratching post, a kitten or cat sometime may be forgetful. When you catch your pet misbehaving, give him a stern reprimand and take him to his scratching post. If he uses the post, praise him lavishly. Correction is only useful if done while the cat is misbehaving. Shouting at your cat after the deed is done and he's off on another caper is a waste of time. He won't understand why you're upset with him and certainly won't learn anything from the experience. But consistent, firm correction during the inappropriate act, and praise for good behavior, will produce the best results.

Authorities argue about the intelligence of animals and their capacity to "understand." Most true animal lovers claim their pets have uncanny human-like emotions. Others disagree, saying that what appears to be comprehension is simply the owner's anthropomorphizing. For example: Do you think a cat can hold a grudge or seek revenge? Although she was embarrassed to admit it, a friend of mine, as a child, had tossed her Siamese into the backyard pool. It was not intended to be a cruel act, simply a childhood prank. My friend soon dismissed the incident from her mind; her cat did not. Several hours later, while preparing for bed, she discovered her pet had soiled her pillow. There are those who would argue the implications of this act, but no matter how you interpret it, my friend gained a new respect for Siamese.

Walking in a Harness

As stated in an earlier chapter, many Siamese breeders will sell their kittens only under the condition that they be strictly housecats. Although cats probably can live perfectly contented lives as such, I feel they should be able to enjoy the outdoors under supervision. The best solution is to train your cat to walk on a leash in a harness. This way your cat can enjoy the sights, sounds and smells of the outdoors, get additional exercise, and you will be present to keep your pet out of harm's way. You won't have to worry about your beloved pet being attacked by a dog or another cat, or meeting an untimely death beneath the wheels of a car. In addition, your cat will appreciate your company.

A cat won't immediately take to your idea of wonderful outings together. Training a cat to wear and to walk in a harness is a gradual process. By the way, I recommend using a harness instead of a collar. Direct pulling of a collar that has been fastened around a cat's neck may harm him.

Training

You may begin this training when your cat is several months old. Start your lessons by allowing your pet to wear the harness around the house for short periods of time. He probably won't like it but will eventually become accustomed to it. You may attach the leash to the harness at this stage and try short ventures around the house.

Siamese are very intelligent, sensitive, and loyal to their owners; these characteristics make them perfect candidates for training.

Be patient, calling your cat's name and pulling softly on the leash. Once the cat seems to be getting the idea, you may take him outside in the evening. Cats are more comfortable in the dark when outdoors. Let him sniff and survey his surroundings. Don't overtire him the first night —a few minutes will do. Gradually extend the evening outings, and when he seems at ease and looks forward to them, you may start taking him for walks during the day.

Don't leave your cat tied to a tree unsupervised. This setup could be less advisable than allowing him to roam free. You'd be taking away one of his greatest defenses—flight. If he were attacked he'd be at a great disadvantage. Besides, walking is good for both of you!

Carriers

Your cat should learn to travel in a carrier. Carriers are invaluable when traveling to shows or to the veterinarian's office. Some veterinarians require them. There are many varieties available on the market. Some cats vociferously object to carriers. Perhaps this is because as kittens they had not been

Training

accustomed to being in one; when as adults they are suddenly closed into one, they voice their unhappiness.

Regardless of the cat's feelings in the matter, he should learn to accept the carrier. When introducing a cat to anything new, you should make every effort to do it while he's young. Let him investigate the carrier, keeping him in it for short intervals while talking to and comforting him. He should adjust to it. The same procedure can be followed with an older cat, but it may take a little longer.

Extended Lessons

Because of his almost canine desire to please his owner, the Siamese can learn many of the same tricks a dog can learn. Many love to play fetch. Others have been taught to jump through a hoop on command, pray, sit and stay, even kiss eyelashes. In some ways they even outshine dogs. Many are adept at opening doors, food containers and drawers. It's up to the owner to decide if these endeavors should be encouraged or discouraged.

More than one Siamese has learned to use the toilet. Some have been taught to do this; others have learned on their own.

The possibilities are endless when working with a Siamese. Some owners are not interested in having a performing cat, while others spend countless hours with their entertaining felines. The potential is there; the choice is yours. If you are interested in teaching your cat more than proper feline etiquette, remember: be firm, gentle, patient and consistent. Enjoy!

The Healthy Cat

Finding a competent veterinarian is essential to any pet owner. Since many of them specialize, it is important to find one who is knowledgeable about cats. I prefer to do my research before actually acquiring a new pet. After receiving recommendations from other concerned animal lovers and checking the yellow pages of the local phone directory for veterinarians who handle the type of animal I'm about to buy, I schedule an appointment for the first week the pet comes to live with me. You would be wise to do the same with your new kitten.

Rapport with your veterinarian is very important. If you have selected one who is knowledgeable but aloof in manner, seems indifferent to your pet, or uses difficult medical jargon which leaves you totally confused, don't feel obligated to stay with him. A veterinarian is an important part of your animal's life and therefore of yours. You should always feel comfortable about asking your vet questions. If you feel you're rushed through appointments, or are dissatisfied with the service, by all means, find another vet, one who shows interest in your kitten and respect for your concern.

I own several different types of animals and therefore deal with more than one veterinarian. This way I'm assured my pets are receiving the best possible care. If I'm ever uncertain about a diagnosis or course of treatment, I get a second opinion (or several, if necessary). The health of my pets is very important to me as I'm sure the health of yours is to you. Don't hesitate to be selective when choosing a veterinarian, and ask as many questions as you need to. Vets have been trained to share their knowledge, so make the most of it. The better informed you are, the better pet owner you will be.

Signs of Ill-Health

Since you are bound to pay a good deal of attention to your Siamese, you should be able to notice if he's not acting quite himself. Some signs of ill-health are loss of appetite, diarrhea, a

The Healthy Cat

coat lacking luster, and film over the eyes. If your cat ignores your presence (certainly unusual for a Siamese), it may mean he's not feeling well. Call your veterinarian if your cat shows any signs of feeling under the weather. He may be able to prescribe treatment over the phone or the situation may warrant a check-up. Don't make your own diagnosis and treat your pet with medicine meant for humans, especially aspirin substitutes. Many of these contain a mild pain reducing compound called acetaminophen, which can be fatal to cats. Regular aspirin can also be very dangerous.

Don't ignore symptoms of ill-health by assuming they will go away in a day or so. You can spare your cat needless suffering with early diagnosis and treatment.

Feline Leukemia Virus (FeLV)

FeLV is a virus which inhibits a cat's natural immune system for fighting off disease and infection. An FeLV-positive cat becomes susceptible to other infectious diseases. Some veterinarians, upon diagnosing FeLV, recommend euthanasia as prognosis for recovery from FeLV is very poor, and it is a highly contagious disease.

FeLV is transmitted through saliva and urine. An infected queen can also spread the disease to her fetus or nursing kittens. Because FeLV is found in the bloodstream, cat fleas and mosquitos may also transmit the disease. Transmission also occurs from biting, scratching, licking, and sharing dishes or litter boxes used by an infected cat.

Although FeLV is a serious concern for cat owners, it should be stated that it is possible for a cat to be infected with the virus and not get leukemia. Apparently, some cats develop antibodies to the virus.

Cats are tested for FeLV with a simple blood test. To protect your cat you should take the following preventive measures:

—Only buy a kitten which has been tested and is FeLV-negative.

The Healthy Cat

—Don't expose your cat to other cats, particularly strays.

—If you purchase a second cat, have it tested before you bring it into your home.

—Test a tom or queen before breeding.

—If you have lost a cat to FeLV, discard all of its belongings, disinfect the household, and do not bring another cat into your home for at least 30 days.

—If you own several cats and one is FeLV-positive, test all of the other cats immediately.

I do not want to create a panic about FeLV, for actually it is not widespread in the general cat population. However, cat owners should be aware of its existence and take the proper precautions.

Feline Cardiomyopathy

Heart problems in cats are rarely mentioned because they are not too common. However, among purebred cats, Siamese (and Persians) are the most susceptible to Feline Cardiomyopathy, which affects the heart muscle and weakens the heart's functions. Males are more often afflicted than females, though only one in a hundred cats is diagnosed as having the disease. Unfortunately, the cause is unknown. Signs to watch for are: difficulty in breathing (due to fluid-filled lungs), abnormal heartbeat, bluish gums, general lethargy, and loss of appetite.

There are three forms of the disease which affect different age groups. The most common, hypertrophic, affects young and middle-aged cats. Older cats may be burdened with dilative cardiomyopathy, while the rarest form, restrictive, generally affects middle-aged cats.

Although there is no cure, prescription drugs, a low-salt diet, and restricted exercise will allow the ailing cat to live a less debilitating life.

Panleukopenia

Also known as feline distemper and infectious enteritis, panleukopenia is a highly contagious disease which affects bone marrow and the intestinal tract. It is 90% fatal among young, unvaccinated cats.

Therefore, kittens should be vaccinated at eight weeks, twelve weeks, and once every twelve months thereafter.

Signs of distemper are high fever, vomiting, diarrhea, loss of appetite and weakness. The disease is spread through saliva, urine, feces, or vomitus.

Distemper can be treated with antibiotics, vitamins, blood transfusions, fluids, force-feeding, and, antidiarrheal and antiemetic medicines. However, prognosis is poor. If you lose a cat to distemper, discard all of its belongings, disinfect the house, and do not bring another cat into your home for several months.

Rhinotracheitis

Rhinotracheitis is an upper-respiratory infection which primarily affects the eye lining and upper breathing tubes. It is usually found in kittens, though older cats are not immune.

Symptoms are nasal and eye discharge, sneezing, fever, red throat, coughing, and drooling. Preventive vaccines are essential and should be administered at eight weeks, twelve weeks, and once every twelve months thereafter.

Calicivirus

Calicivirus is another respiratory infection which primarily attacks the mouth and lungs. Symptoms are similar to those of rhinotracheitis; additionally, ulcers on the tongue, nostrils or roof of the mouth may be present. An infected cat will act severely depressed.

All three of the foregoing diseases can be prevented with a combined injection FVRCP (Feline-viral-rhinotracheitis-calicivirus-panleukopenia) at the ages previously described. Prevention of these illnesses is imperative, as they are all serious and life-threatening.

Pneumonitis

Pneumonitis has symptoms similar to those of the other respiratory infections together with the addition of red, bloodshot eyes and bloody nasal mucous discharge. Inoculations should be given at twelve weeks, nine months, and fifteen months of age. (NOTE: There is a vaccine known as the "4 in 1" which acts to immunize panleukopenia (feline distemper), rhinotracheitis, calicivirus and pneumonitis. The "4 in 1" is administered at four, seven, ten and fourteen weeks. Many breeders and their veterinarians prefer this method of vaccination. Others prefer the FVRCP inoculation described above and vaccinate against pneumonitis separately and at different ages. How and when to administer vaccinations is a highly subjective area of concern. The methods described in this book are meant to act as a guideline only and to emphasize the importance of vaccinations. If you have established a relationship with a veterinarian you trust, rely on his advice.

Rabies

Rabies is a viral disease that affects the brain. There has been a steady increase in the number of rabies cases in cats. Since 1981, the reported number of cases in the cat population has outnumbered those of dogs, probably because cat owners, in the past, have not typically had their cats inoculated for this dreaded disease. Rabies can be transmitted to humans and has a high (nearly 100%) fatality rate. Although some humans have recovered through supportive therapy, animals are not treated due to the severity of the disease and its consequences.

Some signs of rabies are unusual behavior ranging from complete lethargy to extreme excitedness, dilated pupils, drooling, and paralysis. Vaccinations are given between three and six months of age and once a year or once every three years thereafter, depending on the particular vaccination. It's essential for indoor as well as outdoor cats to be vaccinated.

Parasites (External)

The four external parasites which could attack your cat are

The Healthy Cat

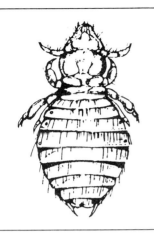

Pesky parasites such as the biting louse (which has been greatly magnified here) can annoy your pet and damage its coat, as the animal continuously scratches itself in frustration.

Parasites (Internal)

There are several different kinds of internal parasites (worms) which could plague your cat. Each of these needs a specific treatment. If you suspect your cat has worms, don't buy a de-worming medicine and treat the animal yourself. A product will be useless if it is not designed to rid your pet of the specific worms involved. Instead, notify your veterinarian who will probably request that you bring him a sample of the cat's stool. By examining the fecal specimen,

the flea, louse, mite and tick. They are referred to as external because they prey on a cat's skin, feeding off blood and tissue fluid. Not only are these pests a nuisance; they can also carry disease.

If your cat persistently scratches and bites at his skin, he could be harboring external parasites. Consult your veterinarian. Treatment varies depending on the type of parasite. In order to prevent recurrence, the cat's living quarters (and possibly the entire house) should be thoroughly cleaned.

The tapeworm attaches itself to the lining of the cat's intestines and then proceeds to feed off its host. If you notice light-colored segments in the cat's stool or clinging to the cat's anus, notify your veterinarian

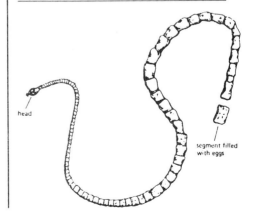

head

segment filled
with eggs

he can determine what type of worms, if any, are present. The proper treatment will then be recommended.

Signs of worm infestation are: slight or severe diarrhea (which may be bloody), loss of appetite or voracious appetite, and a bloated stomach. Worms live in the cat's body and literally feed off it. Left unattended they can be a serious problem.

Cystitis

Cystitis, a urinary tract inflammation, is fairly common. It is caused by urinary calculi, diet, infection, and, sometimes, a body chill. Signs are: frequent urination, though only a few drops of urine may appear, straining in the litter box, or complete disregard for the litter box. Because cystitis is very painful, your pet may cry when it attempts to urinate.

Cystitis can usually be cleared up with antibiotics. However, if the condition is serious, surgery may be necessary. It is not unusual for cystitis to recur, as there is no complete cure.

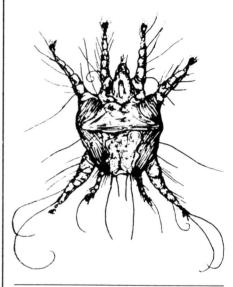

Head shaking and ear scratching may be signs of ear mites in your cat. Above is a single ear mite (greatly magnified).

Hairballs

Hairballs are created in the stomach when a cat swallows a lot of hair from self-grooming. Siamese are less apt to develop hairballs than the long-haired breeds, but it is possible.

Vomiting may solve the problem, but if the hairball has become enlarged and is blocking the digestive tract, other measures are needed. Lubricants, such as petroleum jelly and

The Healthy Cat

mineral oil, administered orally may help, or there are commercial products available on the market. In severe cases, surgery may be necessary. Frequent grooming on your part will help prevent hairballs.

Eczema

Eczema is a word used to describe nonspecific skin irritations. Causes are not fully known, but there are two varieties, moist and dry. A cat afflicted with moist eczema will have a wet discharge in a certain spot which will become pimply and scaly. With dry eczema, the moist area dries up, causing an irritating itchy patch, which may spread.

Eczema comes on suddenly and must be treated by a veterinarian. When a cat is diagnosed as having eczema, it means all other specific skin ailments have been ruled out and the true nature of the problem is not known. Treatments may be given internally or externally and are often required for an extended period of time.

The Danger of Houseplants

There are several reasons why cats may opt to chew on houseplants: curiosity, boredom, or the need for roughage (an unproved theory) are just a few. No matter what the reason, the consequences can be deadly serious, as some plants are highly toxic.

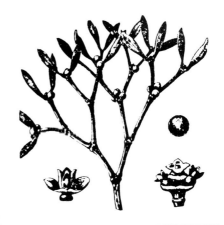

There are quite a number of plants that can be poisonous to felines, including the berries of the mistletoe.

You have several options for keeping your cat out of harm's way: a) cat-proof the house, that is, place plants in spots impossible for the cat to reach; b) train your cat to ignore plants; c) buy only plants known to be nontoxic; d) grow your cat his own greens; and e) don't bring plants into your home.

If your cat has nibbled on a poisonous plant, bring the cat and the plant (for easier diagnosis) to the vet immediately. Some signs of poisoning are: vomiting, diarrhea, convulsions, loss of coordination, labored breathing, rash and coma.

A few houseplants known to be poisonous are listed below:

Ivy
Philodendron
Marigold
Christmas Cherry
Mistletoe
Poinsettia
Oleander
Daffodil
Hyacinth foliage

(NOTE: In some cases only the fruit of the plant is believed poisonous; in others the entire plant is.)

Captions for color photos on pages 57-64.
Page 57: A beautiful head study of one of the Dei-Jai cats, owned by Bill and Doris Thoms of Dei-Jai Cattery. Page 58, top: Julia Koestler with her lynx point pal. The kitten is owned by Dr. Robert C. Koestler. Page 58, bottom: CFA Grand Champion Cannoncats Abelard, a seal point male, showing excellent color and type. Owned by Virginia A. Cannon. Page 59: Solid-colored Siamese are known as Oriental Shorthairs in some cat registering associations. Here Grand Champion Saroko Cafe Noir, owned by Dr. Robert C. Koestler, nurses her kitten. Page 60: A Saroko kitten owned by Dr. Robert C. Koestler of Saroko Cattery. Page 61: Profile shot of Double Champion Kim-Kee's Loki of T-Lu, a lilac point owned by Janet R. Beardsley. Page 62: J-Bars Maid Marion of Saroko, an eight-month-old red point female owned by Dr. Robert C. Koestler, in an aristocratic stance. Page 63, top: Eight Siamese and Colorpoint Shorthair kittens. Owner, Robert C. Koestler. Page 63, bottom: Champion Lur-O-Luv Lady Danae of Delian and her ten-day-old litter. As the kittens mature, their markings will darken and become more evident. Owners, Dolores and William Kennedy. Page 64: At a cat show, judges will assess the Siamese chin and jaw as part of their overall evaluation of the animal.

The World of Cat Shows

Cats have been domesticated for thousands of years. Yet many established breeders may find it hard to believe that the world of pedigrees and show cats has existed for just over 100 years. To the average cat owner, it may come as a surprise to learn that an organized cat fancy even exists. The cat fancy includes all people who love and show cats, especially those who devote themselves to the welfare and breeding of pedigreed cats.

In the late 1800's, Harrison Weir, a British artist, cat lover and Fellow of the Horticultural Society, designed the first organized cat show. Though cats had been shown at fairs and exhibitions, Mr. Weir had greater aspirations. He wanted to enhance the appreciation of cats with respect to breeds, colors, markings, etc. He created the first "Points of Excellence," or standards, to be used in judging cats, along with a cat show schedule, classes, prices, and prizes. Next, he approached Mr. Wilkinson, manager of the Crystal Palace in London, a large exhibition hall built entirely of glass, to hold his show. The Palace had been used for various types of shows and exhibitions, including dog shows. Permission was granted. On July 31, 1871, the first cat show was held. Mr. Weir, his brother John Jenner Weir, and the Reverend J. Macdona acted as judges. There were 160 exhibits. The show was a huge success and became a model for worldwide cat shows; the enthusiasm created by the show set off the cat fancy as we know it today.

At CFA shows Siamese are now classified in Group II, which includes breeds with similar body type rather than coat length.

65

The World of Cat Shows

The original shows consisted of shorthaired cats, classified by color. They were judged on a scale of 100 (the "Points of Excellence") which were divided by characteristics related to the overall appearance of the cat. Those of greater importance, the head, for example, were worth more points than the tail. Some standards have changed very little over the years, though they may differ from organization to organization. Of course, when new breeds are introduced, new standards are established.

Because of the success and popularity of the early cat shows, it was recognized that in order to create a cat of a specific color, knowledge of parentage was needed. In 1887, the National Cat Club was formed, headed by Harrison Weir. The club started a stud book and thus it became the first registering body for pedigreed cats. It continued in this capacity until 1910, when the Governing Council of the Cat Fancy was formed and took over the registration responsibilities. However, the National Cat Club was allowed to have four delegates on the Governing Council. Meanwhile, cats were shipped from Britain all over the world. The first official American cat show was held at Madison Square Garden in New York City in 1895.

Today, several cat associations make up the North American cat fancy. The CFA (Cat Fanciers' Association) is the largest. Because opinions will always differ as to what constitutes a breed, how many generations are needed to adequately trace a pedigree, and what the ideal should be for each breed of cat, the associations have differing rules and standards. However, their high regard for the ethical development of pedigreed cats is the same and all are useful sources for learning about purebred cats.

The American Cat Association (ACA), founded in 1897 by Lady Beresford, is the oldest of the North American cat associations. The ACA does not have a Colorpoint Shorthair class; all colors are considered Siamese.

The American Cat Council (ACC), founded ten years ago, is in the process of revising its standards and show manual. The

The World of Cat Shows

ACC registers "Household Pets" which can be shown in their own category. Household pets are judged on color, personality and grooming. The ACC considers all colors of Siamese as Siamese.

The American Cat Fanciers Association (ACFA) was founded in 1955 by a dedicated group of cat fanciers who wanted greater flexibility in developing cat breeds. The ACFA is a democratic association. Members vote on all issues relevant to the rules, bylaws and registration rules. Breeders create the Standard of Perfection for their breed. All colors of Siamese are considered Siamese.

The Canadian Cat Association (CCA) was founded in 1961. Prior to that time, registrations were filed in the United States or Europe, and all Canadian shows had to follow the rules of American associations. The CCA was developed to promote the welfare of all cats in Canada, to improve individual breeds and to form a purebred registry. The CCA is governed by a President and Board of Directors who act on the wishes of the membership and report to them each year.

Siamese and Colorpoint Shorthairs are listed as two separate breeds.

The Cat Fanciers' Association (CFA), the largest organization of its kind in the world was formed in 1906. The CFA is governed by an Executive Board which sets the policies of the organization. Changes and suggestions from its member clubs are taken under consideration. The CFA recognizes only four colors of Siamese; all other colors are considered Colorpoint Shorthairs.

The Cat Fanciers' Federation (CFF) formed in 1919 is based on equal representation. The executive board is made up of one delegate or proxy per club. Member clubs submit proposals pertaining to all relevant organizational matters. These ideas are then circulated to all other member clubs. After careful consideration, voting instructions are given to the representative. Decisions are made by the majority vote. The CFF considers all colors of Siamese as Siamese.

The Crown Cat Fanciers Federation (CROWN) founded in

The World of Cat Shows

1965 has brought a new approach to the development of cat shows. Cats registered with other associations may be shown in CROWN shows without being registered in CROWN. CROWN uses a positive approach in judging by presenting cat owners with a rating slip listing all of a cat's good points. This organization considers all colors of Siamese as Siamese.

The International Cat Association (TICA) formed in 1979 has members throughout the world. The association will accept individual members as well as club memberships. TICA is a genetic-based registry which means any possible color within a breed can be registered. For example, the Cinnamon Point, a fairly new Siamese color, has been accepted by TICA. Therefore all possible Siamese colors are considered Siamese in this organization.

The United Cat Federation (UCF) founded in 1946 has only chartered membership; there are no individual members. Every year club delegates meet to elect a new Board of Directors who handle the affairs of the organization. Siamese and Colorpoint Shorthairs are considered separate breeds in the UCF.

If you would like additional information on the various feline organizations, write to *Cat Fancy* magazine or *Cats* magazine.

You should ask your breeder about the associations he belongs to. Also write to the various associations requesting general information and a list of local clubs in your area. As you become more knowledgeable about rules and standards, you can decide which ones are of importance to you. It is not unusual for a cat to be registered in more than one association.

Every cat club in the country is affiliated with one of the associations. When a club puts on a show, it is sponsored by the club's national affiliate and governed by the rules of that particular association. When you attend shows sponsored by different associations you will begin to observe the varying standards and rules.

Clubs promote the welfare of all cats, hold shows, and often invite animal professionals to

The World of Cat Shows

attend their meetings as guest speakers. They may also donate to a local cause such as an animal-welfare organization. Clubs are well worth joining. It's wonderful to be in an atmosphere with others who share your love and interest. I'm always concerned that I will bore my friends with endless anecdotes about my beloved pets. However, others like me can indulge themselves by joining a club whose members really listen and care.

Show people are a dedicated group. They drive long distances to shows and spend long days at show sites, often with disappointing results. Yet, they persevere. What drives them on? The answer I'm sure is a personal one, though few would deny there is an unmatched excitement, joy and challenge in competition.

Understanding Show Competition and National Scoring Systems

Kittens are eligible to participate in shows from the age of four to eight months. This age bracket forms the Kitten class. Siamese kittens of the same sex and color are compared together, the judge selecting the Best and Second Best. He does this with every Siamese color class. (Remember, there are only four Siamese colors recognized in CFA; all other colors are judged as Colorpoint Shorthairs. Several colors are accepted in some of the other associations.) When the "Bests" have been selected from all of the breeds, they are compared with each other. The five outstanding kittens are chosen as winners. If trophies have been donated, they will be awarded to all five winning kittens. Kittens are not permitted to compete for championships.

When a cat is past eight months of age, he is shown as an adult. He is first shown in the Novice or Open class. Depending on which association is sponsoring the show, he could win a first and a winner's ribbon. Different associations require a different number of winners' ribbons to complete a championship. The next step is for all male Champions to be

The World of Cat Shows

compared and the best awarded a "First." The same procedure is followed for females.

When cats have completed all championship requirements in the given association, they may participate in the Champion class. The Grand Champion class is open for those cats who have accumulated the required points for Grand Champion.

When all colors of Siamese have gone through this process and a judge picks a Best and Second Best from all of the colors, then a Best and Second Best are chosen from all colors of all breeds entered. At this point a Best of Breed (or division) is chosen, and then a Second Best of Breed (or division). Then come the finals when the following cats are chosen: Best and Second Best Novice or Open, Best and Second Best Champion, and Best and Second Best Grand Champion. The top five cats are chosen and awarded a rosette.

In addition to the above, all-breed shows include Best and Second Best Longhair, Best and Second Best Shorthair, Best and Second Best Longhair

Champion, and Best and Second Best Shorthair Champion. From these four, the Best and Second Best Champions in the show are chosen.

Some organizations use the aforementioned Top Five system; other organizations use a Top Ten system. When selecting the Top Ten, a judge picks the Best through 10th Best from the Best and Second Best previously selected. There is also a Best and Second Best Champion. Rosettes are awarded to these cats as well.

Altered cats may also participate in cat shows in a separate class. They are often called Premiers. The scoring system follows the same procedure as that of the unaltered cats.

All of this information may seem rather confusing at first, but as you observe more shows, talk with knowledgeable cat fanciers and extend your reading of the subject, you will find it really is quite fascinating. You will discover, too, that judges look for more than just a well-proportioned cat. They check all parts of the body, including firm muscle tone and a healthy skin

The World of Cat Shows

and coat. Cats are allowed to be vocal while being shown, but nipping automatically disqualifies them. Also, squints and kinked tails are serious show faults in Siamese.

Tips For The Novice

Novice cat fanciers should not jump into the show world at full speed. It is far better to enter gradually, learning as much as possible before actually buying your first show kitten. Attend as many shows as possible, speak to knowledgeable people in the fancy, read as much about cats and showing as you can, familiarize yourself with the rules and regulations of the various associations. In other words, do your homework! Owning and showing cats can be very satisfying; it can also be expensive and disappointing. The uninformed buyer may be taken advantage of when purchasing his first show kitten if he doesn't know what to look for. Often the novice expects too much when he first enters the fancy.

Once you have followed the shows, researched the various bloodlines (becoming aware of both positive and negative traits), and have some idea of the difference between pet, show and breeding quality, then you can buy your first show cat. Many breeders recommend starting with a neutered male. That way you won't have to deal with a male's spraying or the pressure of selecting the mate for your male or female. Living with breeding cats can be very demanding, as they are often destructive, expensive and noisy.

If you enjoy showing your Premier and feel ready to get more involved, buy the best female kitten you can find. Don't expect too much in the first year or so. Remember, cat showing, with the proper attitude, can profoundly change your life all for the better.

Breeding

By now it should be obvious that breeding is a serious business. I don't use the term "business" to refer to an occupation (though it may be in some instances) but to emphasize the time, the devotion and the financial commitment involved in breeding purebred cats. Ethical breeders have carefully considered the satisfaction as well as the sacrifices involved in breeding. They go to great lengths to keep their cats healthy and content, constantly striving to improve their bloodlines and making every effort to find good, loving homes for their kittens. People who allow their pets (males as well as females) to roam free to breed indiscriminately, or those who arrange to have their Siamese bred with the "Siamese-looking" cat owned by a neighbor do a great disservice to the animals and to those dedicated to improving the breed.

All cats are very sexually motivated, the Siamese exceedingly so. Females come into heat as early as six to eight months; however they should not be bred until they are at least twelve months old. Males show signs of sexuality at six to twelve months, but are usually not used for breeding purposes until they are eighteen months old. For those who have never been exposed to a Siamese cat's sexual behavior, the experience can be more than a little unnerving. The female will become very restless; she seems to twitch all over and rolls about on the floor. She'll crouch and paw with her back feet and "call" or scream at an unbelievable pitch. The male sprays (squirts urine) indiscriminately at almost any vertical object. This act, which cannot be repressed, is highly objectionable in the home. (Owners of cattery studs may allow males wearing stud pants out of their cages for additional exercise.)

The female's periods of heat usually last five to seven days, but this frequency differs from cat to cat. Some come into season once a month, others once every two to three months. Unfortunately, some "call" for weeks with only a short rest period between each heat. When the male reaches sexual maturity,

Breeding

Bobbed Tail

Straight and Tapering

Small Kink

Long, Long, Double Kink

Hook Tail

Curled Tail, Rigid

Double Kink

Show-quality specimens should exhibit long, tapering tails. Any evidence of a kink is cause for disqualification.

Breeding

he can impregnate the female in heat at any time. Cats that have not been altered and are not bred can develop both psychological as well as physiological problems. Surely, the owner, too, will suffer. Therefore, if you simply want a companion, it really is best to have your pet altered. She will not become fat and lazy as many erroneously believe, and the procedure will not have a negative effect on personality. If anything, personality may improve because the cat will not be preoccupied with sex.

If you have weighed all the factors and responsibilities, and are now convinced that you want to get involved in a breeding program, do go about it in the proper manner.

Finding the Stud

You spent a good deal of time researching catteries and bloodlines when you purchased your female kitten—now you'll want to do the same in order to find a worthy stud. Because breeders always want to improve upon the cats they already have,

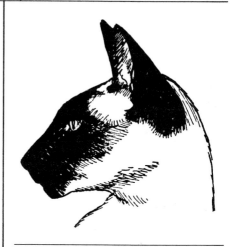

If you are breeding show animals, look for those Siamese that have excellent type according to the breed standard.

finding a stud of good type is very important. Study bloodlines carefully; be aware of positive as well as negative traits in the different lines. Learn as much as you can about genetics. Become familiar with the terms Inbreeding, Linebreeding and Outcrossing. In general, Inbreeding refers to mating closely related individuals, such as mother and son, or brother and sister. Linebreeding involves inbreeding through several generations, mating relatives that are not as closely related, i.e., aunt to nephew, uncle to niece.

Breeding

Outcrossing is the breeding of unrelated cats. You should also discuss breeding prospects with several knowledgeable Siamese breeders.

When you find a cat you're considering as a stud, be sure to study his pedigree. You'll want to know if his ancestors also have the desired traits you are trying to attain by using this particular stud.

The Proper Procedure

When you have settled on a stud, you and the owner of the stud should discuss all terms before the actual mating takes place. Usually the owner of the male will want a stud fee. The price will reflect the male's show status. Or sometimes, instead of a fee, the owner of the stud will take a kitten from the litter in place of the fee. He may want the pick of the litter, second best, or possibly prefer a female to a male, etc.

When the terms have been agreed upon, make arrangements to leave your queen when she is in heat at the home of the stud.

Males more than females like to be on their home ground for romantic interludes. Be sure your queen is in good health and clip her nails, as she may strike out and harm the male. Usually the queen will stay with the stud for a few days, so they will have an opportunity to mate more than once. If for some reason the queen does not become impregnated, you'll have to bring her back. So be certain that arrangements for a second rendezvous are included in your original agreement. If all goes well, you can expect the litter in 63 to 66 days (about nine weeks).

Delivery

Two weeks or so after being bred, a queen may vomit for a few days. Don't panic. She is simply experiencing morning sickness. You won't notice any other signs of pregnancy until about four weeks, at which time her nipples will become larger and pinker. At five weeks and beyond, you will see a steady increase in the size of her abdomen.

Breeding

A few weeks prior to the queen's due date, you should prepare a nest area for her. A large, low box with towels or blankets in it, or the bottom drawer of a dresser, will do nicely. Because cats don't like to deliver in brightly lit areas, be sure to select a spot where you can control the lighting. Your cat will probably prefer to find her own nesting place, but you should try to get her to accept the set-up you have arranged so you will have easy access to mother and kittens during delivery, should they need your assistance. In order to acquaint the queen with the nesting box, place her in it for a few minutes every day and lavish her with affection. Hopefully, she will get accustomed to it and accept the arrangement. However, Siamese are very adept at finding their own nesting spots despite your efforts. If this does occur, don't worry. You can always move the new family to the prearranged area afterwards.

The Siamese queen does not want to be alone as her due date nears; she will follow you more persistently than ever. Though

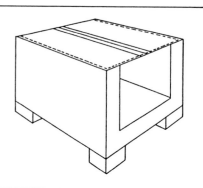

A large, clean, sturdy cardboard box serves well as a nesting box. By raising it off the floor a bit, you will help keep drafts and dampness out of the nest.

cats can deliver unassisted, it is wise to make your veterinarian aware of your queen's condition and make sure he or an associate will be available if complications arise that you cannot handle.

When your queen is about to deliver you will see a mucous discharge; then her water will break. Kittens are normally delivered head first encased in a sac of liquid, though breech births (feet first) are not uncommon. The queen should clean the kittens, chew the umbilical cord off and eat the afterbirth. If this is your first

Breeding

KITTENING CHART

JANUARY

Mated	01 02 03 04 05 06 07 08 09 10 11 12 13 14 15 16 17 18 19 20 21 22 23 24 25 26 27 28 29 30 31
Kittens	7 8 9 10 11 12 13 14 15 16 17 18 19 20 21 22 23 24 25 26 27 28 29 30 31 01 02 03 04 05 06

MARCH   APRIL

FEBRUARY

Mated	01 02 03 04 05 06 07 08 09 10 11 12 13 14 15 16 17 18 19 20 21 22 23 24 25 26 27 28
Kittens	7 8 9 10 11 12 13 14 15 16 17 18 19 20 21 22 23 24 25 26 27 28 29 30 01 02 03 04

APRIL   MAY

MARCH

Mated	01 02 03 04 05 06 07 08 09 10 11 12 13 14 15 16 17 18 19 20 21 22 23 24 25 26 27 28 29 30 31
Kittens	5 6 7 8 9 10 11 12 13 14 15 16 17 18 19 20 21 22 23 24 25 26 27 28 29 30 31 01 02 03 04

MAY   JUNE

APRIL

Mated	01 02 03 04 05 06 07 08 09 10 11 12 13 14 15 16 17 18 19 20 21 22 23 24 25 26 27 28 29 30
Kittens	5 6 7 8 9 10 11 12 13 14 15 16 17 18 19 20 21 22 23 24 25 26 27 28 29 30 01 02 03 04

JUNE   JULY

MAY

Mated	01 02 03 04 05 06 07 08 09 10 11 12 13 14 15 16 17 18 19 20 21 22 23 24 25 26 27 28 29 30 31
Kittens	5 6 7 8 9 10 11 12 13 14 15 16 17 18 19 20 21 22 23 24 25 26 27 28 29 30 31 01 02 03 04

JULY   AUGUST

JUNE

Mated	01 02 03 04 05 06 07 08 09 10 11 12 13 14 15 16 17 18 19 20 21 22 23 24 25 26 27 28 29 30
Kittens	5 6 7 8 9 10 11 12 13 14 15 16 17 18 19 20 21 22 23 24 25 26 27 28 29 30 31 01 02 03

AUGUST   SEPTEMBER

JULY

Mated	01 02 03 04 05 06 07 08 09 10 11 12 13 14 15 16 17 18 19 20 21 22 23 24 25 26 27 28 29 30 31
Kittens	4 5 6 7 8 9 10 11 12 13 14 15 16 17 18 19 20 21 22 23 24 25 26 27 28 29 30 01 02 03 04

SEPTEMBER   OCTOBER

AUGUST

Mated	01 02 03 04 05 06 07 08 09 10 11 12 13 14 15 16 17 18 19 20 21 22 23 24 25 26 27 28 29 30 31
Kittens	5 6 7 8 9 10 11 12 13 14 15 16 17 18 19 20 21 22 23 24 25 26 27 28 29 30 31 01 02 03 04

OCTOBER   NOVEMBER

SEPTEMBER

Mated	01 02 03 04 05 06 07 08 09 10 11 12 13 14 15 16 17 18 19 20 21 22 23 24 25 26 27 28 29 30
Kittens	5 6 7 8 9 10 11 12 13 14 15 16 17 18 19 20 21 22 23 24 25 26 27 28 29 30 01 02 03 04

NOVEMBER   DECEMBER

OCTOBER

Mated	01 02 03 04 05 06 07 08 09 10 11 12 13 14 15 16 17 18 19 20 21 22 23 24 25 26 27 28 29 30 31
Kittens	5 6 7 8 9 10 11 12 13 14 15 16 17 18 19 20 21 22 23 24 25 26 27 28 29 30 31 01 02 03 04

DECEMBER   JANUARY

NOVEMBER

Mated	01 02 03 04 05 06 07 08 09 10 11 12 13 14 15 16 17 18 19 20 21 22 23 24 25 26 27 28 29 30
Kittens	5 6 7 8 9 10 11 12 13 14 15 16 17 18 19 20 21 22 23 24 25 26 27 28 29 30 31 01 02 03

JANUARY   FEBRUARY

DECEMBER

Mated	01 02 03 04 05 06 07 08 09 10 11 12 13 14 15 16 17 18 19 20 21 22 23 24 25 26 27 28 29 30 31
Kittens	4 5 6 7 8 9 10 11 12 13 14 15 16 17 18 19 20 21 22 23 24 25 26 27 28 01 02 03 04 05 06

FEBRUARY   MARCH

Breeding

litter, you may want an experienced friend there to assist if the mother has trouble with a breech birth or does not clean the offspring. Siamese usually have four or five kittens, but it's not unusual to see a few more.

When all the kittens are born, replace wet bedding with clean, dry towels, and place a bowl of water down for the mother. Then leave the new family alone to rest and get acquainted.

The New Kittens

During the first four weeks, the queen is totally in charge of her kittens. Your responsibilities are to keep the nesting box clean and see that the mother is well fed and healthy. She should receive extra calcium and additional food during pregnancy and lactation. At four weeks you should start the kittens on a prepared diet and feed them four or five times a day.

From six weeks on, your kittens will delight and amuse you. A home once enlivened with the spirit of one Siamese now abounds with activity and mischief. You may find it difficult to part with your kittens, but finding them good, caring homes is very important. You may decide to keep a favorite kitten for yourself! Remember to retain kittens until they are four months old so their new owners will have all the advantages you had when you purchased your first Siamese.

Suggested Reading

Look for other T.F.H. books to help you with the selection and care of your Siamese cat and to give you further reading pleasure. All titles listed here are available at pet shops and book stores everywhere.

CAT BREEDING by Dagmar Thies. Contents include: A Guide for Potential Breeders. Biology and Genetics. Building up a Breeding Stock. Practical Advice from a Practitioner. The Cat Fancy.
ISBN 0-87666-863-5
TFH KW-065
Hard Cover, 5½" x 8", 128 pages

CAT CARE by Dagmar Thies. Contents include: The Cat in Changing Times. Buying a Cat. Maintaining a Cat. Caring for a Cat. Cat Breeding as a Hobby.
ISBN 0-87666-862-7
TFH KW-064
Hard Cover, 5½" x 8", 96 pages

CAT OWNER'S ENCYCLOPEDIA OF VETERINARY MEDICINE by Joan O. Joshua, F.R.C.V.S. Contents include: The Cat—Pet and Patient. Functional Anatomy of the Cat. Restraint, Sedation, and Anesthesia. Signs of Health and Disease and Routine Clinical Examinations. The Alimentary Tract. Respiratory System Including Diaphragm. Cardiovascular System. Urinary Tract. Reproductive System. The Skin. The Skeletal System. Nervous System. Diseases Due to Infective Agents. Geriatric Care. Some Common Accidents and Injuries Including Poisoning.
ISBN 0-87666-856-2
TFH H-985
Hard Cover, 5½" x 8", 320 pages

ENCYCLOPEDIA OF AMERICAN CAT BREEDS by Meredith D. Wilson. Contents include: Abyssinian. American Shorthair. American Wirehair. Balinese. Birman. Bombay. British Shorthair. Burmese. Chartreux. Colorpoint Shorthair. Egyptian Mau. Exotic Shorthair. Havana Brown. Himalayan. Japanese Bobtail. Korat. Maine Coon. Manx. Manx Longhair (Cymric). Oriental Shorthair. Persian. Ragdoll. Rex. Russian Blue.

Suggested Reading

Scottish Fold. Siamese. Somali. Sphynx. Tonkinese. Turkish Angora. Color Standards.
ISBN 0-87666-855-4
TFH H-997
Hard Cover, 5½" x 8", 352 pages

SHORTHAIRED CATS by Harriet Wolfgang. Contents include: Introduction. Acquiring Your Cat. Diet. Training. Grooming. Travel. Your Cat's Health. Safe Play. Breeding. Care of the Queen. Selling. Cat Breeds. Exhibiting Your Cat.
ISBN 0-87666-180-0
TFH H-920
Hard Cover, 5½" x 8", 190 pages

SIAMESE CATS by Ron Reagan. Contents include: To the Prospective Cat Owner. Common Sense Cat Care. Ailments and Afflictions. First Aid. Breeding. Queening. Siamese Varieties. ACFA Standard.
ISBN 0-87666-860-0
TFH KW-062
Hard Cover, 5½" x 8", 128 pages

THIS IS THE SIAMESE CAT by Marge Naples. Contents include: History of the Siamese Cat. The Show Standard for Siamese Cats. How to Buy a Siamese Kitten. Choosing His Name and Registering Your Kitten. Training Your Kitten. Grooming. Feeding Cats and Kittens. Health of Your Kittens and Cats. Catteries. Stud Cats and Queens. Motherhood and Kittens. Breeding. Cat Associations and Clubs. Shows. Show Competition and National Scoring Systems. Siamese Lore.
ISBN 0-87666-853-8
TFH PS-617
Hard Cover, 5½" x 8", 256 pages